TYNISHA C. LEWIS

31 Days To
NOTHING MISSING NOTHING BROKEN

OBTAINING PEACE IN A CHAOTIC WORLD

Copyright Notice

31 Days to Nothing Missing, Nothing Broken:
Obtaining Peace in a Chaotic World
by Tynisha C. Lewis, BA, JD

© 2021, Tynisha C. Lewis, BA, JD
www.TynishaLewis.com
info@tynishalewis.com

Published by:
Anointed Fire House
www.anointedfirehouse.com

Cover Design by:
Anointed Fire House

Author photograph by:
John Washington, Jr./JWJ Photography

ISBN: 978-1-955557-03-0

This book contains material protected under International and Federal Copyright Laws and Treaties. Any unauthorized reprint or use of this material is prohibited. No part of this book may be reproduced or transmitted in any form or by any means, electronic or mechanical, including photocopying, recording, or by any information storage and retrieval system without express written permission from the author/publisher.

I have tried to recreate events, locations, and conversations from my memories of them. To maintain their anonymity in some instances, I have changed the names of individuals and places, and I may have changed some identifying characteristics and details such as physical properties, occupations, and places of residence.

Although the author and publisher have made every effort to ensure that the information in this book was correct at press time, the author and publisher do not assume and hereby disclaim any liability to any party for any loss, damage, or disruption caused by errors or omissions, whether such errors or omissions result from negligence, accident, or any other cause.

Scripture quotations marked NIV are taken from The Holy Bible, New International Version ®, NIV ®, Copyright 1973, 1978, 1984, 2001 by Biblica, Inc.™ Used by permission. All rights reserved.

Scripture quotations marked NLT are taken from The Holy Bible, New Living Translation, Copyright© 1996. Used by permission of Tyndale House Publishers, Inc., Wheaton, Illinois 60189. All rights reserved.

Scripture quotations marked ESV are taken from The Holy Bible, English Standard Version®. English Standard Version is a registered trademark of Crossway®.

Dedication

This book is dedicated to Aiden, my son. He came into my life when I needed him the most. He unknowingly pushed me to keep going during the last 11 years of his life. My resilience is partly because of his existence. So, to Aiden, let's keep going together.

Even when I am no longer here with you and times get rough – hold God's hand and KEEP WALKING.

I love you, Aiden.

Thank you to my family. There are too many of you to name, but being a Gibbs/Cohens made me who I am.

I love you all.

Acknowledgments

Thank you, God, for helping me through the trials and triumphs. Also, thank you, God, for your Son, Jesus.

Thank you, Jesus, for going to the cross for me.

Thank you, Holy Spirit, for being my internal Comforter and for walking alongside me.

Thank you, Life, for throwing things at me that allowed me to see how much God truly loves me and for showing me how He will flip things upside down just to provide for and protect me.

Thank you to the pastors and spiritual leaders I have had over the years of my life:
Bishop Otis A. Floyd
Bishop Eddie L. Long
Bishop Paul S. Morton
Apostle Marquis Boone
Pastor Alex Brown

and my mentor,
Tiffany Buckner, a.k.a. "Anointed Fire"

Welcome

I have gone through storms. I have gone through fire. I have had to run through walls. I have had to break through glass ceilings. I have had to navigate through very bumpy terrain.

Evictions. Repossessions. Insufficient funds. Sickness. Death of a loved one. Divorce and loss of romantic relationships. Termination of employment. Low self-esteem. Friends walking away. My enemies were coming close. My family was feuding.

I have experienced all this.

New home. New car. Increase. Health and wellness. Spiritual family. Great friendships. Business innovations. Healthy confidence. Godly relationships. Victory over my enemies. Restoration in the family.

I have experienced all of this as well.

Through it all, God was with me. Even when I could not specifically trace Him, He was there whispering these encouraging words to me that I now share with you.

How To Use This Devotional

Read this devotional one day at a time so you can fully digest the contents. Pray before each reading. Grab a notebook, take notes and strategize on how you can apply these principles to your life. Find yourself in the daily devotions and determine what areas you can move toward a greater life, both spiritually and naturally.

Table of Contents

How To Use This Devotional IX

Day 1 ....
    Approve Yourself 1

Day 2 ....
    Too Much Access 3

Day 3 ....
    Fully Activated 5

Day 4 ....
    I'm Am No Longer Afraid 7

Day 5 ....
    Confusion/Disorder Is Not from God 11

Day 6 ....
    You Can't Have My Peace 13

Day 7 ....
    Don't Be Scared to Be Different 17

Day 8 ....
    Toxicity Is Contagious...................................21

Day 9 ....
    Go Where You Are Celebrated.....................23

Day 10 ....
    Squad Goals..25

Day 11 ....
    I Am Not Perfect, But I Am Willing 29

Day 12 ....
    You Are in My Business 33

Day 13 ....
    Do I Have Your Attention! 37

Day 14 ....
    Called. Equipped. Qualified. 41

Day 15 ....
    More For You Than Against You 45

Day 16 ....
    High Quality vs. High Quantity......................47

Day 17 ....
    The Joy of The Lord Is Your Strength 53

Day 18 ....
    Quick Response 57

Day 19 ....
    Try Jesus 61

Day 20 ....
    Fully Mature 65

Day 21 ....
    Can't Compete Where You Don't Compare .69

Day 22 ....

Keep Your Eyes on The Prize 73

Day 23 ....

Zero Games..77

Day 24 ....

Be True To You 83

Day 25 ....

The God You Serve Is Mighty 87

Day 26 ....

Forgive or Forget 91

Day 27 ....

Let My Yes Be Yes and My No Be No..........97

Day 28 ....

Faith It Until You Make It 101

Day 29 ....

Come Out Of Confusion 105

Day 30 ....

Final Destination 109

Day 31 ....

See Yourself 113

Day 1

Approve Yourself

Romans 8:1 - There is therefore now no condemnation to them which are in Christ Jesus, who walked not after the flesh, but after the Spirit.

Seeking the approval of other people allows those people to have too much control over our lives. As a result, it is likely that at some point, we will compromise and do things that we would not normally do. We may compromise by walking outside of God's will for the approval of people. Have you ever been there? I have. Unfortunately, when we finally obtain the approval we so desire, we can lose ourselves while sustaining that approval.

How do we refrain from losing ourselves trying to win the approval or opinion of others?
- ✓ Step 1. Know who YOU are.
- ✓ Step 2. Know what YOU value.
- ✓ Step 3. APPROVE YOURSELF!

Many people go through life trying to gain approval through their clothes, the houses they purchase, the educations they obtain, and many other identifiers. What if I told you that you are already approved? God has endorsed you! He has approved you so much that He said that if you choose Christ, you shall no longer have to go through life seeking people's approval. By the mere fact that you decide to walk after the Spirit of God, He approves you and what you do. You have approval already, so there is no need to pursue it. And if the God of all creation approves you, why would you need the approval of anyone else? Remember this the next time you decide to compare yourself to another individual or you decide to tell yourself, "I'm not good enough." You are more than good enough. You are APPROVED!

Day 2

Too Much Access

Matthew 13:57 - And they were offended in him. But Jesus said unto them, A prophet is not without honor, except in his own country, and in his own house.

When people have too much access to you, they start to think you are regular. Do you ever wonder why it may be hard to get those closest to you to support your vision or believe in whatever God is doing in your life? It's because they are familiar with you. They grew up with you. They played outside with you. They think they know you fully. They don't know that God has done something new in you. It has sprung forth, and they don't even see it. It's okay. They don't need to see what God has changed about you. Your tribe will see it and appreciate it! The people in Jesus' hometown were offended when He became public about who He was and what His goal was. Isn't that Mary's son? Isn't He just a

Carpenter? They could not see that He was and is THE GREAT I AM.

You've been processed, true enough, but everyone will not understand or acknowledge your process. That's fine. Your process was not for "them" because, truth be told, they desire to stay where they are. You were processed to connect with others who wish to grow with you. Every healthy tree loses leaves that no longer serve a purpose during the Autumn, but soon Spring arrives, and a new set of vibrant leaves replace the ones that fell. (Do you see where I'm going with this?) I encourage you to personally ask God to let every dead thing in your life be replaced by new, fresh, and vibrant versions. You have never been and will never be *regular*.

Day 3

Fully Activated

James 1:6 - But let him ask in faith, nothing wavering. For he that wavereth is like a wave of the sea driven with the wind and tossed.

When it feels like something has died (relationships, friendships, and opportunities), this is typically the time for something new to be birthed. That failed relationship, that job termination, that broken friendship, that bankruptcy, that repossession, that negative health report—these things are all too often the catalysts and the boosters we need for our FAITH to be FULLY ACTIVATED!

We learn about God through Bible study, books, and tradition, but EXPERIENCING God for ourselves is another scenario. For example, when you're about to get evicted or your car is scheduled to be repossessed, and the money comes right on time. You now KNOW Him as a Provider. Or when the doctor has given you or a loved one a diagnosis, but the prayers of the righteous availeth much, and you or that loved one fully recovers from the illness or disease. You now KNOW him as a Healer. Faith is more than believing that God can do it. Faith is being confident in God's ability to do it for YOU. If God is God – pray and ask Him for what you desire and believe (do not doubt), so you can RECEIVE what is yours. So many things are a part of our birthrights as Believers. We have a right to healing. It belongs to us. We have a right to prosperity. It belongs to us. We have a right to godly relationships. They belong to us. All these things belong to us, and our confidence must coincide with God's desire to give these things to us.

Day 4

I'm Am No Longer Afraid

Philippians 4:6-7 Be anxious for nothing, but in everything by prayer and supplication, with thanksgiving, let your requests be made known to God; and the peace of God, which surpasses all understanding, will guard your hearts and minds through Christ Jesus.

Don't let the enemy use FEAR against you! Don't run from the fight. RUN TO THE FIGHT!!! (The good fight of faith, that is.) The enemy has a way of influencing us with fear by presenting situations that have not occurred and probably won't ever occur! He continually presents us with worst-case scenarios. What if my business fails? What if I will never find love again? What if my idea falls flat? He throws all kinds of negativity at our minds, and when this happens, we catch and accept some of those things to be true. What if I told you that you don't have to accept every idea that seeks to enter your mind? What if I told you that you

31 Days to Nothing Missing Nothing Broken

could recognize negative thoughts, and if they do not line up with the Word of God, you can cast them down?

You do not have to accept every negative thought that seeks to bombard your mind. You can intentionally create thoughts that go against the voice of the enemy and align your mind with what God is saying about your life. Instead of thinking, "What if it fails?" begin to think, "What if it works?" What if the business becomes a million-dollar business? What if the ministry flourishes and blesses millions of people? Begin to have a conversation with yourself and cast down those thoughts that do not line up with God's will and His Word for your life. "The weapons of our warfare are not carnal, but they are mighty for the pulling down of strongholds" (2 Corinthians 10:4). We can pull down strongholds such as anxiety, worry, and fear. So, the next time you become fearful, begin to use your weapons. Our weapons include but are not limited to: The Word of God, prayer, fasting, communicating with other Believers, reading inspirational books, and watching online videos/sermons about faith and how to cancel fear.

31 Days to Nothing Missing Nothing Broken

Our weapons are plentiful and powerful. Pick one (or all of them)!

Day 5

Confusion/Disorder Is Not from God

1 Corinthians 14:33 – For God is not the author of confusion but of peace…

Have you ever tried to put an area of your life in order, and all of a sudden, that area got even more chaotic? God is not the author of confusion (or disorder), but the enemy is. I remember when I was trying to get my finances in order. I began to track my spending and saving. That's when things started to go haywire concerning my finances. It seemed like I started spending more on outside food and entertainment when I had groceries at home. I was trying to come out of a system of confusion/disorder surrounding my finances, but as you may know or you may soon find out, systems of confusion don't easily let us go.

So, I had to do something I had never done. I wrote out all my bills and income. I also began to use online bookkeeping software to track how I spent my money. The more and more I practiced these functions, the more I came out of confusion or disorder surrounding my finances. We can apply these principles to every area of our lives.

Where there is confusion, there is typically something that is preventing us from hearing the voice of God about the situation. It could be a multitude of things. We sometimes ignore the seriousness of our bad decisions. But when we realize the areas of confusion in our lives, we can better plan how we will come out of those chaotic places. When we no longer accept confusion, we will do what we need to do to change. This means that we will begin to question the way we function. We will begin to pursue understanding about our issues. We will find people who have successfully navigated through those areas and try to learn from them. Eventually, we will desire the consistent removal of the confusion in any area of our lives. That is when our lives will better reflect God's perfect will.

Day 6

You Can't Have My Peace

Philippians 4:7 – And the peace of God, which surpasses all comprehension, will guard your hearts and your minds in Christ Jesus.

Every day, there are so many things that try to take our peace. From losing our keys to bumper-to-bumper traffic, maintaining our peace is often a tug-of-war battle. Some of the people we meet in person, some who call us on the phone or contact us on social media, come with the assignment, knowingly or unknowingly, to steal our peace. They try to steal our peace, and in exchange, leave us with fear by sharing the big breaking news story about COVID-19. They try to steal our peace by sharing gossip about other people. They try to steal our peace by calling us with their "emergencies," thinking they should become our "emergencies." Again, people will try to steal our peace – intentionally or unintentionally.

We must set boundaries around our lives and let people know that our peace is OUR PEACE, and no one can have it. Sometimes, it is not people; sometimes, there are situations that seek to steal our peace. Thinking about too many issues or thinking negatively about those issues can steal your peace. Many things can cause us to simply hand over our peace, including whispers about layoffs around the workplace or when our spouses/significant others begin to act irrationally. To keep our peace, we must consistently renew our minds by reading the Word of God. Reading the Word of God will help us train our minds to stay focused on God, His promises, and the awesome peace associated with believing and implementing His promises. We don't have to hand over our peace to people, circumstances, or situations.

Today, let's make an intentional effort to obtain peace, and not only get it but KEEP it. We can maintain our peace by asking God to help us recognize everything that tries to steal our peace and by asking Him how to manage our peace using the greatest amount of wisdom. Additionally, let's ask God how to address people who try to steal our peace. We must ask Him how to confront the people who try to steal our peace and how to do so peacefully. Keeping our minds on the things of God will result in the peace of God flooding our lives, which will guard our hearts and minds with the Spirit of God.

Day 7

Don't Be Scared to Be Different

1 Peter 2:9 KJV - But ye are a chosen generation, a royal priesthood, a holy nation, a peculiar people..."

Wearing different color hair and certain hairstyles were viewed as weird. Fast-forward to today—those same colors and styles are now commonplace and popular. What do you know?! What was deemed different or weird has become very much liked by many. This is a good example of why we should not be afraid of being different. Stepping out into a new industry, business, relationship, or venture that does not look like anything that has ever been done before can be intimidating. Many times, we get revelations from the Spirit of God, but because what He shares with us is very different, we sometimes dismiss the ideas and move on to more familiar territory.

What we are familiar with often becomes the very thing that we attract. However, we tend to ignore or not even consider the new things God whispers to our spirits. God chooses us; this is why we are peculiar. So, it is only to be expected that we will have thoughts and ways that are peculiar to some people, and that is perfectly alright! We are creative innovators, and we introduce new, fresh, and groundbreaking ideas to the world. Remember, our God saw the Earth, and it was void. He then spoke new and different things into it, including, "Let there be light." The light was new and different. Once God called forth light, the light was obligated to exist. The same is true with us. When we receive downloads of new ideas and thoughts, we should not avoid or dismiss those ideas. If you have a different fashion style, explore that! Don't say to yourself that your fashion choices look nothing like what your friends and family members wear. That's not necessarily a bad thing! You could be onto something new! The point is that you don't need to fear what people have to say about your differences.

The best deliverance we will ever experience will be the deliverance from the opinions of people. The opinion of others can be one of the biggest obstacles to overcome, but it is doable. Once we focus on what God wants from us and what He wants to do in our lives, all other opinions and hearsay lose their power and importance. When God spoke light, He did not ask for anyone's opinion. When God spoke our destinies, again, He didn't ask for anyone's opinion. With that being said, go be great and go be different!

Day 8

Toxicity Is Contagious

Proverbs 22:24-25 - Make no friendship with a man given to anger, nor go with a wrathful man, lest you learn his ways and entangle yourself in a snare.

We take the trash out every day because it has no use, plus, it smells foul. Yet, we allow toxic people to linger in our lives. I'm not calling people trash. As Believers, we love people. However, ever so often, we can identify people who give off offensive smells, spiritually speaking. Let me explain. People who verbally abuse, degrade, manipulate, or treat us offensively are what I call toxic people. Other toxic people include:
1. People who secretly compete with us.
2. People who wait to see our faults so they can exploit those faults.
3. People who disrespect us and call us out of our names every chance they get.

4. People who speak against or try to minimize what we accomplish.

These are people who we need to love from a distance. For whatever reason, these people seek to pour (or spew) toxicity into all interaction with us. In most of these instances, we can decide whether we want to deal with these people or not. However, many times, fear keeps us in these toxic relationships. We are sometimes fearful of confronting issues and/or drawing boundaries. As a result of not seeking God's will, we sometimes remain in abusive, traumatic, or degrading experiences longer than we need to. We can say no to toxicity, abuse, and trauma. Those negative experiences do not have to be ours. We must assess the people who come into our lives and determine for what reason they have come. We must create healthy boundaries, and we must require people to respect our boundaries. Or we have to offer them the door to exit our lives until they can respect those boundaries. We won't get mad. We won't be full of strife. We will just recognize that God's highest and best for us does not include dwelling in a place of toxicity, abuse, and trauma.

Day 9

Go Where You Are Celebrated

Matthew 10:14 KJV - And whosoever shall not receive you, nor hear your words, when ye depart out of that house or city, shake off the dust of your feet.

Have you ever had someone discount your value? For whatever reason, they were unable or did not want to recognize your value. It could have been envy, jealousy, or plain ignorance—they just didn't know. Either way, the God of all creation has deemed us valuable. Therefore, the opinions of people rank below the opinion of God.

So, what does God say about us? He said that before we were born, He valued us. Before we earned any awards, titles, or accolades, God was genuinely in love with us. Before our spiritual glow-up, He knew us when our spirits were ugly, and He remained in love with us. So much so that He gave His ONLY

Son, Jesus, to be crucified for our sins. He gave up one of His most valuable possessions in exchange for us. Knowing this, how can we doubt our value? God has already stamped us as VALUABLE. God has already declared that we have great worth. So then, why do we listen to the voices of people knowing that they have less authority, less rank, and less power than God? He has certified us as WORTHY! We have been stamped as VALUABLE. So, then all other contrary opinions have absolutely no weight when it is all said and done.

Day 10

Squad Goals

Psalms 91:11 KJV - For He shall give His angels charge over you, to keep you in all your ways.

You have Heaven and all its resources backing you. Now, act like it! At some point, we will find ourselves feeling alone as Believers. Even when we have family and friends all around us, there comes a point in our lives when we feel like people don't understand us or people disagree with the direction we are heading. There are seasons when we feel like there is no one we can call on, nor is there anyone we can reach out to for encouragement or advice. The truth of the matter is that there is ALWAYS someone listening to you. His name is Jesus. But, understandably, as humans, we want human companions and friends.

In our search for companionship and friendship, it is a great idea to ask God to show us the people we need to connect with. We need to ask Him for a new mindset to attract and identify quality friends who will contribute to us being spiritually productive and prosperous. God wants to be involved in every aspect of our lives, including who we choose to partner with as friends, companions, and business partnerships. In His infinite wisdom, God can share with us what decision would be best in the short and long run. It is an excellent idea to ask God which direction to go in when dealing with other people. Remember, He knows the hearts and intentions of everyone. He can see the spiritual forces that we are unable to see. For example, I remember when I was dating a guy who would just flatter me ALL the time. He would tell me how beautiful I am, and he would just flatter me in a very excessive, extraordinary way. When I took the situation to God in prayer, He revealed that all that flattery was because the guy wanted something from me and he wanted it quickly. You can use your imagination to guess what he wanted from me. I almost fell for it, but thanks be to God that He opened my eyes to see what was not being shown and opened my ears to hear what was not being said.

Praying about the people who enter our lives is what we, as Believers, should often do. Asking God about the people who enter our lives is a great way to avoid a lot of bad decision-making. Ask God to reveal any hidden agendas or ulterior motives that people have. Ask God if it is a good idea to keep specific people around. When we make it a practice to inquire of God (and listen to what He says), we will begin to make very good decisions when it comes to the people we connect with. Remember, we want our squad to be squad goals - FOR REAL!!

Day 11

I Am Not Perfect, But I Am Willing

Philippians 3:12 AMP - Not that I have already obtained it [this goal of being Christlike] or have already been made perfect, but I actively press on so that I may take hold of that [perfection] for which Christ Jesus took hold of me and made me His own.

Before we were babies in our mothers' wombs, God had already fallen in love with each of us. He never said, "I will love them when they do everything right." In all our imperfections, we were still considered *enough* for God to give His only Begotten Son to be crucified for our sins. God doesn't expect us to do everything perfectly. He knows that we are prone to sin because we are wrapped in flesh. Sin is a part of our innate nature, but once we are born again and accept Christ as our Savior, we can work out our salvation by walking according to the Word of God and cooperating with the Holy Spirit. We then go on a life-long journey towards *holiness* AND *wholeness*.

Many people are under the assumption that they must get everything right before they come to God when, in actuality, things begin to fall in line once we come to God. The characteristics and habits (sins) that we do not have control over - lust, anger, lying, and greed - begin to lose their grip as we walk closely with God and experience His power. All too often, we try to fight our battles alone, thinking that we have enough human strength to fight spiritual forces. That's pride! As humans, we cannot defeat the dark forces, principalities, and spiritual wickedness in high places that surround us daily. Our enemy, Satan, continuously tries to influence us with various sins through television, music, and people. However, we have the Holy Spirit to help us remain in agreement with God concerning our actions and attitudes. God knew that we would need some help. After Christ's crucifixion, the Holy Spirit was sent to us to guide and support us. If we agree with God and earnestly try to make decisions that align with His Word, we will be pleasing to God, not perfect, but pleasing. In the areas where we fall short, the

Holy Spirit will come alongside us and help us when we are willing to accept His help. This is the key – we must be willing to accept God's help, and then we will see continuous progress. Not perfection, but progress.

Day 12

You Are in My Business

Proverbs 3:5 - Trust in the Lord with all your heart, and do not lean on your own understanding.

Don't be afraid to trust God with YOU. He is concerned with every area of your life. Let me ask you a question. Has it ever been easy to believe that God would do something for someone else, but you have a hard time believing that God will do what you need to be done? It is amazing how we can have enough faith for everyone else. We pray for everyone else. We fast for others. We expect a breakthrough for our friends and family members. It is almost as if we believe God will do what He does, but we don't believe He will do it for us particularly. Have you ever been there? I've been there. The truth of the matter is that God is not a respecter of persons. His Word is equally applicable to all Believers. Whether you have a title in the local church or not, your faith is what makes it possible for you to please God.

It does not benefit us to have faith in God for one area of our lives, but not to have faith in God for all areas of our lives. Knowing that it is His will that we prosper, have good health, and have a soul that prospers, why do we find it so difficult to take God at His Word? I'll tell you why. We have had people *drop* us in life, meaning some of the people we thought should have cared simply did not. Or the love that we wanted was not given to us. In some of those instances, those people did the best they could with what they had, but we found what they gave was very much less than what we needed. We then took that insecurity into our relationship with God. When we enter a relationship with God, He wants our full confidence and trust in Him. He doesn't want us to waiver and go back-and-forth with whether we believe Him or not. He said it! We believe it! That settles it! Yes, I know that's easier said than done, but that is how it should be.

Trust and confidence are necessary for us to walk in agreement with God. We must believe that not only will He do it, but that He will do it for us. We cannot misplace the disappointment we have experienced with people onto God. He is not a man that He should lie, and He is not the son of man that He should repent. That means when He says it, you can be 100% confident that it will happen, but in His timing. Remember, God is sovereign, and He consults with no one concerning our destinies and what He wants to get out of our lives. When we became Believers, we became His instruments; we became His tools for the advancement of His Kingdom. We will not allow our lack of faith to prevent His will from happening on the Earth. We will work on our faith by practicing His presence through worship and praise, reading and listening to His Word, praying, fasting, and interacting with other Believers. This is how we grow our faith in God, not only for others, but also for ourselves.

Day 13

Do I Have Your Attention!

Romans 8:31 - What shall we then say to these things? If God be for us, who can be against us?

Take your eyes off who wants you to fail and place your eyes on God. Honestly, everyone will not like us. There will be people who dislike us, and we won't know why. It may be an unclean spirit inside of them that causes them to dislike us, or it could be their insecurities. It could be several reasons why certain people refuse to like us, but we cannot become too consumed with their opinions. We can't allow our lives to revolve around who likes us versus who doesn't like us. If our ways and attitudes reflect God's nature, we can't be concerned with the people who choose not to be our friends or associates. Occasionally, we will come across people who seek to be our enemies. They want to harm us either mentally, emotionally, or even physically. All the same, there are many instances in the Bible where Believers had to defend themselves against actual, tangible enemies.

For example, at some point, Elijah found himself up against Jezebel's henchmen, about 400+ prophets of Baal. During his conversation with his opponents, Elijah proclaimed that God was on his side. When Elijah called fire from Heaven, God burned up an altar soaked with water, demonstrating that He heard Elijah's prayers. Jezebel also sought to have Elijah physically harmed, but ultimately, Jezebel's team threw her from a window to her death. After which, dogs ate her body.

The point is that many of the enemies that come against us cannot harm us because of God's ability (and willingness) to protect us. Read that again. Our enemies have plenty of bark, but very little bite. We serve an omnipotent and almighty God who protects us and does not allow our enemies to obtain victory over us. When all of Heaven, including angelic hosts, God, Christ, and the Holy Spirit, are on our side, they will cause even our enemies to be at peace with us. When our enemies come against us, the wisest thing for us to do is to pray, hold our peace, follow the instructions of God, and let Him fight our battles. This may not be the solution in *every* instance, but it is the solution in *many* instances. God said vengeance is His; this means that we do not have to fight against every person who comes against us. Sometimes, the best response is to hold our peace and not respond. We do not have to cuss people out. We do not have to get an attitude. We do not have to run to the phone or social media to slander our enemies. Praying during contentious times can help us discern when it is time for confrontation and when it's simply time for relaxation, trusting in God's ability to handle our enemies.

Day 14

Called. Equipped. Qualified.

Philippians 1:6 - Being confident of this very thing, that He which has begun a good work in you will perform it until the day of Jesus Christ.

When we were young, God began to work in our lives. He had already mapped out how He would use our life's experiences, our education, our upbringings, and all the events of our lives. He knew that He would use the good and bad experiences to bring about His will for our lives and the lives of people we impact.

So, the question is, why do we sometimes feel insecure about how our lives are going? I understand that sometimes we make bad decisions, and as a result of those decisions, we experience negative consequences. Those negative experiences may lead us into seasons where we do not trust God as we should be.

Overall, God has already considered our mistakes, our downfalls, the times that we will miss the mark, and the many times that we will do things that do not please Him. God took all of this into consideration, and He still loves us! He still calls us close to Himself. For example, before being named Paul, Paul was named Saul, and he murdered Christians. For some reason, God knew that He could take Paul's zeal and use it for His glory. God did just that. Paul, the same man who murdered Christians, also became the man who wrote more than half of the New Testament. The Spirit of God very much inspired Paul's teachings, and even today, we still look to many of the things that Paul wrote for guidance as Christians.

In our insecurity, we sometimes look at people and say in our minds, "I could never accomplish that!" When what God has put inside of us empowers us to accomplish "that" and more! We have to get past ourselves and be stretched in our relationship with God. We often look at ourselves as insignificant and unworthy. It could be because the people we should trust, for some reason or another, disappoint us and make us feel unworthy. That is the story of many of our lives. Whether our parents, relatives, romantic interests, or teachers, there was an instance (or many instances) where we felt we could no longer trust people to have our best interests at heart. We then displace that feeling of mistrust and disappointment onto God, even though He said that NOTHING will separate us from His love. NOTHING that we do, have done, or will do, can separate us. NOTHING that other people can do, have done, or will do can separate us from His love. God walks with us through the most complex struggles of our lives. He loves us so much that He wrote a love story that we call the Holy Bible. He gave us instructions, standards, and He answered our questions—all in the Bible! We just have to take the time to read His love letter to us. Why is He so in love with us? This is a great question. What was God thinking when the love letter was being written? He wants us to find the treasure that is His heart, so He left the treasure map. He has not only called us, but He has also equipped and qualified us to walk out the entire purpose for our lives. We find out more and more about that purpose the further we dive into the Word of God.

From this point forward, do not feel insecure about your life! Your life has value, and your life has worth. God wants to use you to bring His will to pass in the Earth. It could be feeding the hungry. It could be paying for someone's housing expenses. It could be cleaning the bathroom at the local church. It could be writing the book or movie that will bring many to Christ. It could be praying for our relatives. It could be showing love to someone who has no one else to care for them. It could be calling to check on someone who just lost a loved one. It could be praying for teenagers that they would make the right decisions in life. There are so many things that God calls us to do. All of these things do not involve holding a microphone and standing in front of multiple people. Some of the things that God calls us to do are intimate and amongst only a few people.

So, just know this, God has called you! God has equipped you! And God has qualified you! Now, go forth!

Day 15

More For You Than Against You

Romans 8:31 KJV - What shall we then say to these things? If God be for us, who can be against us?

Has it ever seemed like the world was against you? Have you ever felt like every and any enemy, both natural and spiritual, were coming after you? The sickness came after you. Lack came after you. Depression came after you. Brokenness came after you. Evil people came after you. YOU came after YOU.

I want to submit for your consideration that we have God, Christ, the Holy Spirit, and angelic hosts sharing in our consistent well-being. What does this mean? Health is ours. Abundance is ours. Joy is ours. Wholeness is ours. Protection is ours. A healthy self-image is ours. All of this belongs to us! These things are our inheritance. These things are our birthrights as born-again Believers. These things belong to us!

We have more going on FOR us than AGAINST us—at ALL times. Even when it feels quite the opposite. Stresses of life can weigh us down, but it is at that time that we can call on God to help us. How can we get God to respond to us? First, having faith that He will respond to us is key. When we cry out to God, He will answer us. Through our praise and worship of Him, God responds. When we read the Bible, we find God, and He responds to us.

Ultimately, God has not left us without direction. But we must seek Him and draw near to Him, and in response, He draws near to us.

Day 16

High Quality vs. High Quantity

Ephesians 3:20 NKJV - Now to Him who is able to do exceedingly abundantly above all that we ask or think, according to the power that works in us.

I knew a businessman who decided to start his consulting firm. His business survived with one client for an entire year before he acquired his second client. How did his business thrive with one client for an entire year? Well, that one client happened to have signed a $150,000 contract with the businessman. My point is I've been asking God to arrange the circumstance to where I connect with high-*quality* people instead of a high *quantity* of people.

The **quality** of our relationships should be far greater than the **quantity** of our relationships. The quality of our relationships speaks to the people and their loyalty, integrity, trustworthiness, and ability to genuinely be interested in our well-being. The quantity is directly related to the number of people we place in the friendship/relationship category.

In this age of social media, the number of followers, subscribers, and friends are significant to some people. There is a sense of accomplishment when your social media followers and friends have reached the thousands on Instagram, YouTube, Twitter, Snapchat, and Tik Tok. However, in real life, we must be concerned about the *quality* of our real friends. Relationships are a significant part of the roadmap to success, both spiritually and naturally.

When I practiced law, I came across quite a few cases where people found themselves in the most unfortunate situations because of their friends or significant others. For example, I remember a young lady who was sentenced to approximately ten years in prison because her boyfriend was selling drugs out of *her* house. When the police raided her home, his stash of narcotics was hidden in the wall. She was indicted, convicted, and sentenced along with him. She claimed that she had no idea that drugs were being hidden in her home. Unfortunately, that was not a good enough defense.

In another case, a young man got into the car with two of his friends. There was a duffel bag with drugs and guns inside the car. As luck would have it, these gentlemen were pulled over by the police. The two gentlemen in the front of the car (the driver and passenger) denied being the owner of the duffel bag. The young man, who simply wanted a ride, was charged with possession of drugs, possession of illegal firearms, and a whole list of charges, all because of who he chose to associate with.

As a mother, I am very concerned about the people my son will choose as friends as he grows into a man. When I was growing up, I remember some of my friends introducing me to some things that I wish I had not been introduced to. I was a latchkey kid, meaning I often came home to an empty house after school because my parents worked. Therefore, I had a lot of freedom. I exercised that freedom in the wrong way on many occasions. For example, I once invited several male friends from the neighborhood into my home. I had to

31 Days to Nothing Missing Nothing Broken

be in my early teenage years. While I was in one part of the house entertaining a young man, his friends were in another part of my house stealing my stepfather's gold coins, the telephone (yes, the actual telephone), a few packs of Kool-Aid, and some microwave popcorn. I remember so vividly my mother returning home and yelling at me about that missing telephone. I had to tell my mother what happened. So, I watched as she walked up the street to the homes of the young men who were at this gathering I hosted. She had a belt around her neck, and I believe she had every intention of using it. Nonetheless, 45 minutes later, she came back home with all the belongings. This was an excellent example of how the quality of people you surround yourself with can directly impact you and your well-being.

Even as an adult, I have come to understand that the quality of people I allow into my life is directly related to my level of success. From a spiritual perspective, the Word of God says, "Be not deceived, evil communication corrupts good manners" (1 Corinthians 15:33). This means that if you hang around evil people or people who don't have your best interest at heart, the things they say and do can and will impact you negatively. We must be careful who we listen to and who we lend our ears to. The more you listen to a person's words, the more they will begin to impact your thinking. Everyone is a teacher to some degree. They are teaching someone somewhere something. That "something" can either be good and beneficial or evil and corrupt. We must be mindful of the counsel and teachings that we listen to. This includes friendships and relationships. We must be aware of who we allow to plant seeds in our minds.

The people we call friends and those we choose to partner with are very significant tools used to cultivate us as we grow. It is a good idea to regularly assess whether we are growing or if we are shrinking due to the people we associate ourselves with. We should be able to look at our lives and say we are maturing and progressing in the right direction with the help of the people we chose to befriend. This is, of course, in addition to our own efforts to mature. You get my point. If we hang out with a certain type of people, we will likely take upon ourselves some of the characteristics of those people—the good and the bad. Yes, of course, we can make our own decisions, but when we associate with people who are making bad decisions, at some point, the consequences of their decisions may affect us. Just as we are concerned about our actual money, let us also be concerned about our relational currency. We must ask ourselves if our friends are helping us walk in more success, spiritually and naturally, or are they making it easier to walk in the pathway of failure and regret.

Day 17

The Joy of The Lord Is Your Strength

Nehemiah 8:10 - Then he said unto them, Go your way, eat the fat, and drink the sweet, and send portions unto them for whom nothing is prepared: for this day is holy unto our Lord: neither be ye sorry; for the joy of the LORD is your strength.

When 2019 began, no one expected the year to end in a pandemic. No one expected lives to be lost on such a massive level. We didn't expect jobs to be lost at such an alarming rate. In 2019, 2020, and even 2021, as I write this devotional, the world is still feeling the tremors of this pandemic. Things have not quite returned to normal. I still see face masks everywhere I go. I see sanitizer stations posted everywhere so we can sanitize our hands. I see signs in store windows saying, "enter at your own risk of contracting COVID-19." We have lived through one of the most historical (and hysterical) periods known to man. At one point, I witnessed hundreds of people standing in lines to get food and water. Early on during COVID-19, I remember the news reporting that hospitals had so many dead bodies that they could not correctly dispose of them. The more I think about it, this was a very traumatic season for the entire world.

During the pandemic, my family had to move to a hotel because our home flooded. We lived in a hotel room for 60 days while our home was restored. I slept on a very uncomfortable fold-out sofa while I gave my son the bed. Despite all the negative instances associated with this period, I can honestly say I was fortunate enough to grow closer to my family. I gained a newfound appreciation of things like food and water. I began to further appreciate having a healthy, functioning body. I began to further appreciate my sources of income. Above and beyond all of this, I began to appreciate my relationship with God. I found myself praying more. I found myself reading the Bible more. I found myself fasting more. There was not a day that went by that I did not play my favorite worship and praise songs. One song entitled "We Gone Be Alright" by Tye

Tribbett was in heavy rotation. That song kept me focused on God. Listening to that song kept joy in my heart during some of the darkest times. I remember back in the day when the older women in the church would always say, "Keep a praise on your lips and a song in your heart." I found out what that means. It means that during the darkest times of our lives, it is necessary to have praise that just easily flows out of us. That praise creates a circle of spiritual protection around us. Inside that circle is the joy of the Lord, and the joy of the Lord is our strength! Praise and worship are ways to create joy in our spaces. With it, we can tap into the presence of God at any given moment. God said that He inhabits the praises of His people (Psalms 22:3). This means that God is living in our praise. This demonstrates the importance of a lifestyle that includes praise and worship. It's more than going to church. It's more than outreach. It's more than singing in the choir. It is cultivating a personal relationship with the God of all creation. It is walking through the darkest times of our lives and still having a one-on-one connection with our Heavenly Father. It is the ability to ease right into the presence of God. And in His presence is where we find the fullness of joy (Psalm 16:11)!

When traveling through dark times, we should find at least one reason to be joyful. Then find another. Then find another. And watch how things are not as bad as they seem. Frankly, we have been through worse times.

Nevertheless, God can do exceedingly, abundantly, above all we can ask or think. So, ask. But don't only ask, also Believe! God has already shown us time and time again that if we take one step, He'll take two.

Day 18

Quick Response

Isaiah 12:2 - Behold, God is my salvation; I will trust, and will not be afraid; for the LORD GOD is my strength and my song, and he has become my salvation.

One day, I was very concerned about something, so I said out loud, "What am I going to do about it, God?" And before I could finish getting the sentence out of my mouth, I quickly heard in my spirit, "Trust God." The response was so immediate, it kind of shocked me.

If we took the time out to literally sit down and count the number of times that God has come through for us, I'm sure the number would be astounding. For myself, I can think back to car accidents that I managed to avoid because I yelled out the name of JESUS. I can recall an instance when I was at a hotel party, and one of the guys at the party began recklessly shooting at another guy, but glory to

God, I did not get hit. I remember when I was in a club with an ex-boyfriend, dancing in front of a door. The next day, I found out that after we left, there was a shooting, and one of the bullets went right through the very door we had been standing in front of. I remember times when I was living recklessly and engaging in unprotected sexual activity with men, but I never caught HIV or AIDS. I remember times when I smoked marijuana, and thankfully, no one ever put anything "extra" in my blunts. I remember when I would drive 20 or 30 miles more than the speed limit while racing with other drivers. I remember occasions when I would be drunk and wake up in my driveway, not knowing how I got home. I have done some pretty stupid stuff!

I say all of this because through this phase of life, when my stupidity was at an all-time high, God protected me! There were several possible outcomes. Those possible outcomes included me potentially losing my life, DUIs, jail time, or disease, but God saw fit to preserve me for some reason. Writing this book could very well be one of the reasons why He wanted me to stick around. When I look back over my life and see all the things

God has brought me through, I can't help but trust Him. There was a time when I wasn't thinking anything about God; I didn't care about grieving the Spirit of God, but He still saw fit to protect me from myself and dangers I could not see. When I placed myself in very tough situations, He rescued me time and time again. So, for that reason alone, my trust in God is abundant. I trust Him with my life because He spared my life on so many occasions. Nowadays, when I find myself in difficult situations, it's easy for me to trust God in those situations. I can't find an instance where He has let me down, including the times when I was walking in direct disobedience to God. During those times, He did not let me be destroyed, even though I willfully stepped outside the boundaries of God's Word and will. When my disobedience made me fair game for Satan, God still protected me! The difference between Job in the Bible and me (during my disobedient season) is that Job was righteous, and I was simply a church attendee. I did not desire a righteous lifestyle. I wanted to do all the wrong that I wanted to do. Therefore, I got my results. I sowed to my flesh, and from my flesh, I reaped corruption—a lot of it!

When I made an executive decision to live my life more righteously, I began to identify God's protection. I was able to look back at all the times God protected me, preserved me, and did not let me destroy myself. And now that I am on God's side, I recognize the fact that if He chose to protect me when I wasn't paying Him any attention, I can surely trust Him with everything I am today as I purposely seek to grow closer to Him as His daughter. I don't worry as much as I used to about money, my businesses, my child, or my well-being. I even recently had a dream about anxiety in my bloodline and how God delivered me and gave me power over fear.

God cares about everything we care about. And we can trust Him to ensure our safety and well-being. He does not want us to go through life worrying and feeling troubled by the cares of this world. He wants us to experience peace, joy, and live lives filled with spiritual abundance. That is His will for our lives! He has not failed us thus far, and He is not about to start.

Day 19

Try Jesus

John 14:6 - Jesus saith unto him, I am the way, the truth, and the life: no man cometh unto the Father, but by me.

Throughout my life, I have tried to find fulfillment in money, men, and methods. But satisfaction only came when I submitted to Christ - the way, the truth, and the life. Several things are fighting for position in our hearts every single day. Money, relationships, possessions, climbing the corporate ladder, power, and prestige; they all fight for places in our hearts. While these things are enjoyable, at no time should they supersede the position God has in our hearts. The children of Israel were in constant struggle with God because they kept finding things to place high in the hierarchy of their hearts. They would often worship the gods of other people. They even went so far as to create a golden calf so they could worship it. Today, even we, as Believers must be careful about the things that we place higher than God in our hearts.

Some people place heavy importance on marriage, while others place a great deal of importance on having a hefty salary. Another person may place importance on being the best athlete on the team. While those things are not bad in and of themselves, when we, as Believers, begin to place more importance on those things than on our relationships with God, we flirt with idolatry. For example, when people commit suicide because they have lost their jobs or because the stock market has crashed, their decisions to end their lives reveals what was positioned high in their hearts. Wherever we store up our treasures, that's where our hearts are. I am by no means saying that we should intentionally live a life of lack without enjoyment. I am saying that many of the things we accomplish and possess are very temporary. Our possessions will change with different seasons in our lives. I have had several cars repossessed. I have been evicted a couple of times. I can also say that I have lost several jobs before I became an entrepreneur. I can admit that those were some very depressing and fearful times. I did not know what to do. Fast forward to today, and I can say in each one of those instances, I made it through. I was able to either replace those items or I discovered that I didn't need them as much as I thought. Throughout the Word of God, we are continuously shown how God shows up for His people. Whether it be to help the children of Israel fight against other countries or how God supernaturally saved Shadrach, Meshach, and Abednego from a scorching furnace. Then again, consider the fact that He gave David the supernatural strength to kill both a bear and a lion. What am I saying? GOD IS FOR US!

I've personally tried a lot of things to feel fulfilled, and the deception was, for a short time, I felt what I thought was fulfillment. Eventually, the fake fulfillment wore off, and I found myself looking for the next thing to fulfill me. It wasn't until I began seeking God that I found true fulfillment. Regardless of what I possessed or accomplished, I realized that the Father's love is enough for me. And the ironic thing is that once I began to seek God for the fulfillment I wanted, all of those other possessions found their way into my life. How ironic is that?! When I began to seek Him first, all those things got added to me.

As we navigate through life, we must keep our eyes on the prize. That prize being the ability to hear the Father's voice say, "Well done, my good and faithful servant."

It is easy to get distracted by the things of the world. For this reason, we must stay prayerful and pursue God's presence to remain focused on the goal. Distractions may come and go, and we must readily identify them and place them where they belong, and that is not above or before God.

Day 20

Fully Mature

Romans 15:1 - We then that are strong ought to bear the infirmities of the weak, and not to please ourselves.

We did not come to God fully mature, but when we came, then God worked out the details. It is amazing how many Christians have experienced that same grace, but refuse to extend it to new Believers or non-Believers. Truth be told, in the last days, God is going to pour out His Spirit on all flesh. So, do we believe God is powerful enough to bring sinners to repentance or not? Our own lives should answer this question for us, because if someone could rewind the tape to when we used to be heavily involved in sin, what would we see?

You don't have to answer that! But I just want us to think for a moment about when we were deep in sin. We wanted to come out, and we wanted to do something different, but we couldn't because sin had such a grip on us. Do you remember how you would sin and then come to God telling Him that if He got you out of that particular situation, you wouldn't do it anymore? Have you ever had to buy a pregnancy test or Plan B because you were scared that you were pregnant, even though you knew you should not have been having premarital sex? I have! Or, as a young man, have you ever gotten a call from a young lady claiming to be pregnant, and you prayed to God to help you out of that situation? These are just instances that I know people go through regularly.

I can count on my fingers and toes several times over how many times I've told God that if He got me out of a situation, I wouldn't revisit my sin. He would help, but I turned right back around and found myself in the same compromising positions. So, when I come across non-Believers or people who still struggle with serving God, I can't be so quick to turn up my nose and deem them to be lost causes. If we have friends or family members struggling with sin, instead of gossiping about them, we must pray and ask God to help them.

Somebody was praying for us when we were stuck and stagnant in our sins. Whether it was our grandmothers, mothers, spouses, children, friends, or spiritual leaders, someone had us on their mind, and they were praying when they saw that we could not help ourselves. Let us not forget our past (and current) weaknesses. We should never get to the point where we think we have conquered every single issue. Sin is always at our door, waiting to pounce. It's only the protection of God, along with His grace and mercy, that empowers us to have the self-control to not give into sin.

And when our paths cross with someone struggling with sin, it is wise for us to refrain from accusations or finger-pointing. Yes, we can remind them about what the Word of God says, but we should not weaponize the Word of God, trying to beat people up in the spirit. It is with love and kindness that God drew us to Himself. It is with love and kindness that we help draw people to Him also.

Day 21

Can't Compete Where You Don't Compare

Philippians 2:2-4 NIV - Do nothing out of selfish ambition or vain conceit. Rather, in humility, value others above yourselves, not looking to your own interests but each of you to the interests of others.

No one can beat you at being you. You cannot beat the next woman or man at being herself or himself. In other words, there's no need to compare ourselves to other people. Insecurity is bred out of such comparison. If we focus on our God-given assignments, we will surely see our immense value.

Several situations in the Bible show how unhealthy comparison with another person can be; these situations reveal how comparison and competition can destroy our relationships. The relationship between Cain and Abel is an excellent example of how comparison can sneak in and destroy the family relationship (see Genesis 4:1-16). Esau and Jacob are examples of two siblings born into a rivalry (see Genesis 25:19-34). Leah and Rachel compared themselves to each other, and the relationship ended up filled with envy (see Genesis 29:5-35). The story of Saul and David also shows us an example of a relationship where comparison is present between a leader and a soon-to-be leader (see 1 Samuel 15-31). And finally, the prodigal son and his older brother also had a relationship that exemplified comparison (see Luke 15:11-32).

Excessively comparing ourselves to other people is a dangerous thing to do. Primarily because it indirectly says to God that who He has made us to be and the gifts/talents He has given us are inadequate. To place more value on someone else's importance implies that who we are and what we contribute are subpar. Imagine putting your heart and soul into creating something, only for the creation to tell you that it does not like how you created it. Imagine the creation saying that it wishes you would have created it to be something else. I cannot imagine an apple saying to God, "I wish you would have created me as an orange." Apples were created to make apple juice, apple pies, applesauce, and apple cider, not orange juice, orange marmalade, or orange popsicles! Be you. That's enough.

Day 22

Keep Your Eyes on The Prize

Colossians 1:10 - ...so that you may live a life worthy of the Lord and please him in every way: bearing fruit in every good work, growing in the knowledge of God...

When we go after the will of God for our lives, we can expect some distractions. The distractions can look like handsome men, pretty women, job loss, wayward children, worry, disbelief, and the list goes on and on. God wants us to ask Him for wisdom concerning the issues we face. He encourages us to ask for wisdom liberally (James 1:5). This means He will give us wisdom in excess. It logically follows that He will also increase our capacity to receive such wisdom. God will not only change the contents (wisdom) of the containers, but He will also change us, the containers.

Distractions can also look like naysayers or people who don't believe in you or your vision. Recognize that you do have a choice as to whether or not you will listen to naysayers and doubters. I choose to believe what God says about my life. It took a lot of time for me to get to the point where I was no longer concerned with people's opinions. I had to immerse myself in the Word of God literally and allow my faith to be cultivated. From then on, I just began to believe what the Word of God said about me, as opposed to what people said about me.

There are some obvious distractions, and there are some distractions that are not so readily identifiable. For example, we are to keep our minds focused on the things above and not on the things of this Earth. This requires us to focus on the things of God. We are encouraged by the Word of God to seek God's Kingdom first. That's where our focus should be, but sometimes, we get distracted by our desires to acquire possessions and enter relationships. We get distracted by listening to the wrong people. We are not to walk in the counsel of the wicked. Wicked is defined as evil or morally wrong. Nevertheless, how many times do we find ourselves seeking counsel from wicked people? We listen to certain music and we watch certain television shows that we should not entertain. This is the same as listening to the counsel of the wicked. We are charged, as Believers, to meditate day and night on the Word of God so that we can be rooted in the Word and yield good fruit. However, there are times when we meditate on everything else. We meditate on our problems. We meditate on things that are yet to occur. We meditate on how people offend us. We meditate on pop culture and current events. We sometimes meditate on everything except the Word of God.

There was a time when I would just religiously watch the news. There was not a day that went by without me watching CNN just to find out what was going on in the world. Eventually, I recognized that I was not doing what Philippians 4:8 tells us to do, which is to focus on the things that are true, honorable, just, pure, and lovely. My focus was on evil, political upheaval, racial tension, and injustice so much so that I found myself anxious and worried. It was not until I returned my focus to the Word of God, prayer, praise, and worship that my focus became sharper.

Yet another area where we lose focus is how we use our words. Proverbs 18:7 says, "A fool's mouth is his ruin, and his lips are a snare to his soul." We can cause ourselves harm by not focusing on the words that we release from our mouths. Remember that out of the abundance of the heart, the mouth will speak (Matthew 12:34). We must remain focused on how we use our words. Are we speaking life or are we creating death with our words? These are only a few examples of not being focused on our words, and there are so many times in our lives where our focus will determine success or failure.

Today, make a conscious effort to focus on what you think about, what you speak, what you entertain, and how you walk through life. Self-examination will allow you to tweak how you show up in the world. And believe it or not, this little change can shift the direction of your life.

Day 23

Zero Games

Ephesians 4:26-27 - Be angry and do not sin; do not let the sun go down on your anger and give no opportunity to the devil.

My Apostle, Dr. Marquis Boone, once said that he needs friends who are "spiritual, not emotional." That hit me in my spirit!

How many times have our emotions gotten us into trouble? Anger, for example, has prompted us to say or do things that we later regretted. How many days have we spent sad about a certain situation, and it led to depression and almost caused us to forfeit the joy of the Lord? Our emotions can move us into a decision-making process that is not based on logic or long-term results, but more on gratifying our immediate need to emote. Being led by the Holy Spirit instead of our emotions will always result in a far more excellent opportunity for spiritual growth. Being led by the Spirit of God causes us to mature and respond in a way that gives God the glory, and it allows us to maintain our witness as ambassadors of Christ.

There is a common colloquialism that says, "Follow your heart." But scripturally, our hearts cannot be trusted because they are so desperately wicked (see Jeremiah 17:9). So, why would we trust something wicked and, at its foundation, morally wrong?

The Bible was written to assist us in determining the most productive strategy to implement when we face the multitude of decisions we must make daily. I call the Word of God the *Believers' Handbook*. It gives us very thorough instructions about how to function as Believers in this world. If ever there comes a time where we don't know the best decision to make, there will be an answer readily available in the Word of God. The Spirit of God inspired the Word of God (see 2 Timothy 3:16). So, by default, reading the Word of God will expose our spirits to the Spirit of God. Ideally, as we make a habit of reading the Word of God, we then begin to come into agreement as God's Word intertwines with our spirits. We then become more in alignment with the will and ways of God. Ultimately, we become more spiritual and less emotional. Our spirits begin to reflect the Spirit of God.

The Word of God describes Christ as the same yesterday, today, and forevermore (see Hebrews 13:8). We can depend on a high level of consistency associated with God and His Spirit. A person who reflects God's Spirit also functions with a high level of consistency. When I think of a double-minded man who is unstable in all his ways, I think about a person who is tossed to and from based upon his or her emotions. Whereas a person who has been processed spiritually tends to lean more towards what the Word of God says about a matter than his or her emotions. Stability and consistency are two characteristics of the people I choose to come in close contact with, especially those I call friends, companions, and confidantes.

Before Apostle Boone said the "spiritual, not emotional" comment during one of his sermons, I never really took the time to differentiate between emotional and spiritual friends. Since that day, I have applied this as a prerequisite for those I consider friends. As a result, I have found myself in connection with many great men and women. Our relationships are not tumultuous. We don't deal with unbearable levels of strife. There is typically a level of understanding and respect that undergirds our relationships. And overall, our interactions are enjoyable. All because I made an executive decision about the type of people I want to be in close contact with. I took accountability for my circle of influence, and now I am reaping the benefits of great relationships.

It is necessary that, as Believers, we make conscious decisions and remain very intentional about the people we call friends. Friend is a label that cannot be placed on every individual we meet. Some people will be *associates*, some will be *business partners*, some will be our *assignments*, and others may just be people we are destined to meet while passing through life. We must remain diligent in asking God what category we should place people in, and when is it a good time to switch those categories if needed. We should ask ourselves whether the people we consider for close friendships/relationships possess the qualities necessary to have an enjoyable, productive, mutually beneficial connection. Once we begin to ask intentional questions and look at the people we surround ourselves with, I believe our relationships will start to transform and flourish. In many cases, we will experience levels of friendship and intimacy that we have never experienced before.

Day 24

Be True To You

Psalms 139:14 - I praise you because I am fearfully and wonderfully made; your works are wonderful; I know that full well.

I used to work in the beauty industry as a makeup artist, and I served hundreds of women and men. I often came across people who were insecure about their looks and physique. Nevertheless, as a pleasantly plump woman, I had a boatload of confidence. Even on my worst days, I felt confident in my looks and abilities. Now, did I feel like I could lose some weight? Yes! But, I never felt like I was not enough or inferior to another person. I would regularly encourage my clients by posting statuses on my social media pages.

One day, I posted the following:
PUBLIC SERVICE ANNOUNCEMENT: Be your weave-wearing, naturalista, vegan, meat-eating, colored contacts, glasses,

thin, plump, employed, entrepreneurial, woke, asleep, married, single SELF! If they do not like what you represent—YOU'LL LIVE!

In other words, I was emphasizing the importance of being yourself and those who appreciate it—GREAT! Those who do not appreciate it—GREAT! I believe, as Believers, we should have this mindset. We do not all look the same, nor do we act the same or think the same. Our God is what binds us together. So, the minor outward differences should not create division between us, but rather, we should learn to be our unique selves and simultaneously respect the uniqueness of others.

I have visited several churches in my lifetime, and I am often surprised at how segregated churches can be. I have attended churches where 99 percent of the attendees were either Caucasian, African American, or Asian. It was as if the message "our kind only" was being said without being explicitly spoken. In the Body of Christ, there is a lack of appreciation for the uniqueness of others. Many Believers exemplify behavior that leads me to believe that they are not interested in fellowshipping with different people.

The world is already very much a caste system. Whether we use money, race, education, pedigree, or prestige, people use so many determining factors to create superficial boundaries and promote division. When you look at most churches, how are they any different?

If you are what we would call a unique or eclectic person, continue to walk in your uniqueness and continue to let that be a part of your character as you grow in God. Conformity was never a part of Jesus Christ's plan. He purposely sought ways to defeat the status quo.

Additionally, we as Believers should not shun people who do not fit our norm or do not resemble us. We should embrace those who come from various backgrounds and possess multiple diversities. Jesus did that during His ministry here on Earth. He accepted people who did not look like Him and people who did not necessarily subscribe to His ideologies. He accepted them, nevertheless.

We, as Believers, can be some very judgmental and self-righteous people. We sometimes feel like our opinions should reign supreme over all other opinions. Nope, not so! I do not believe that tattoos and piercings will keep people out of Heaven, but many Believers condemn those who have tattoos and piercings as if they are headed straight for hell. Yes, we should share what the Word of God says with those who wish to listen, but our own lives will testify of God before we ever open our mouths. We should be the standard of God. We should not weaponize the Word of God with the intent to assassinate anyone who does not possess the level of godliness we assume they should have. Believers engage in friendly fire all too often. We would rather beat someone down with the Word of God than to allow the love of God to flow from us to other Believers, non-Believers, and new converts. It was with loving-kindness that God drew us—remember? How are you drawing people?

Day 25

The God You Serve Is Mighty

2 Chronicles 20:6 - and said, "O LORD, God of our fathers, are You not God in Heaven? And do You not rule over all the kingdoms of the nations? Power and might are in Your hand, there is no one able to take a stand against You.

"Ohhhh TELL me...WHO can...stand BEFORE us...WHEN we CALL on THAT GREAT NAAAAME?!"

This was a song that I often heard at my previous church. One day, I began to listen to the words and ask myself who is this God that I serve? That when His enemies stand before Him, they are brought to destruction? For me, it began to logically follow that if I am an individual who has dedicated my life to serving God, when enemies rise against me, they too can expect that the God of all creation will come to my defense.

Angelic hosts and warring angels will defend us during our spiritual battles. It is to be expected that when Satan comes against us as Believers, we have an army (a legion of celestial beings) who also come to our defense and aid us. We are not helpless, nor are we at a disadvantage. We have the advantage. We have God sitting high and looking low, paying attention to us. We have Jesus, our continual Mediator, forever defending us. We have the Holy Spirit inside of us, walking along with us, empowering us to carry out the will of the Father. Additionally, we have angels who have been given charge over us. We cannot lose! Even when it seems like we're losing, we are winning because the Word of God says all things work together for the good of them that love the Lord and are called according to His purpose (see Romans 8:28). We love God. We are called according to His purpose. Therefore, all things work together for our good.

There are so many situations in the Bible that demonstrate how God orchestrates defense strategies on behalf of His people.

Gideon.
David.

Joseph.
The children of Israel.
Jesus.

The Word of God includes back-to-back examples of how God defends His people. This is why it is vital to read the Word of God. You will never know how God feels about you as a Believer unless you read the Word of God. While it is a book, it is also a spiritual letter to the people of God. The Word of God shares how God will protect us, provide for us, love us, cover us, and keep us from dangers seen and unseen.

So, to answer the question that the song poses, "Who can stand before us when we call on that great name?"

The answer is NOONE.

Day 26

Forgive or Forget

Proverbs 17:9 NIV - Love prospers when a fault is forgiven, but dwelling on it separates close friends.

Forgiveness means I won't hold the offense against you. Forgiveness does not mean that I am obligated to give you the chance to offend me again. As Believers, we can expect that people will offend us and mistreat us by simply being human beings. But the difference is that the Word of God clearly warns us that there will be times of great persecution in our lives.

Persecution can show up in so many different ways. Persecution can show up as a supervisor who continues to harass you or treat you badly. Persecution can show up looking like a spouse whose behavior negatively impacts your relationship. Persecution, outside of America, can look like losing your life because you chose to be a Christian and follow the Word of God. Persecution can come in several forms, and according to the Word of God, it is guaranteed to come at some point in our lives. When persecution comes, we choose to forgive or hold onto the negative feelings associated with the persecution. "Forgive them, Father, for they know not what they do" are the famous last words of Jesus Christ, our Savior (see Luke 23:34). This is our example to follow.

Forgiveness is one of those things that Peter felt should be done only seven times, while Jesus explained that it should be done 70 times 7 (see Matthew 8:21). So, the revelation is that when we feel as if we have forgiven enough, we have to extend even more forgiveness. We have to stand by God's promise that vengeance is His and allow Him to exact vengeance, not us (see Romans 12:19).

Often, we take things into our own hands. We cuss people out. We have bad attitudes. We ignore and give people the cold shoulder. We "cancel" people and completely evict them from our lives, but the question is, when we do this, are we forgiving people or simply trying to forget people? Are we doing what is comfortable for us by getting rid of people to avoid forgiving them? I agree that there are some instances where it is wise for us to remove ourselves from situations to avoid turmoil and strife. However, there are also situations where we must forgive and still interact with the people we have forgiven. When we must interact with people who we must also forgive, we must pray and ask God for discernment on how to move forward in those relationships. We must pray and ask God to help the other individuals not be as offensive as they have been in the past. We may even need to pray that we are not overly sensitive due to the offense.

One thing about relationships, whether romantic, familial, or platonic, is that we NEED God's insight on how to navigate through them most effectively. It is necessary to understand that every person we meet is not meant to be our friend. Every person we meet is not meant to come in close connection to us. Every person that we meet is not meant to have an extended time in a relationship with us. We have to be wise about how we deal with people. In all honesty, some people have been sent on assignment by Satan to come into our lives and wreak havoc. In the same manner, some people have been assigned by God to come into our lives and be a blessing beyond belief. However, communing and regularly conversing with God will help us to better identify which category each person belongs in. We would not need to extend forgiveness to others as often if we'd consult God more before we entered into relationships. Think about that for a moment.

The Word of God states, "In all your ways acknowledge Him (God)," (Proverbs 3:6). Acknowledge Him concerning friendships and relationships. So, the next time you meet someone, bring that person into your prayers by asking God if the person is someone you should connect to. Additionally, listen to the instructions given to you by God during prayer time! This is the area where a lot of us fall short. When God reveals who a person is, we still want to forge ahead with our agendas, thinking we can re-write the story with our special powers. When those relationships do not work out the way we thought they would, we return to God, broken and sad, refusing to acknowledge the fact that He warned us from the beginning. (Maybe, I am the only person who risked it all, even after being warned). God sees what will happen 10, 15, or 1000 years from now, and He is well able to forewarn us today about the relationships we choose.

Some people may say that asking God about our relationships is "too deep". Others may say it does not take all that, but I wish we could ask Samson how following our feelings can be disastrous. Judges 16 described how Delilah manipulated Samson into revealing that his strength was in his hair, and she took advantage of his confidence by giving him over to his enemies. His feelings for Delilah led him into the bed of betrayal and to his untimely death. How would that story be different if Samson had consulted God about that relationship? Can you relate?

Day 27

Let My Yes Be Yes and My No Be No

Ephesian 4:25 - Each of you must put off falsehood and speak truthfully to your neighbor, for we are all members of one body.

Matthew 10:16 - Be as wise as a serpent but as harmless as doves.

If you have spent any time around people, you have realized that people want what they want. Some people will try to get what they want by any means necessary. By this, I mean people use manipulation, domination, intimidation, or control to get what they want. I'm not only referring to people who are non-Believers, but also those who profess to be Believers. Don't let manipulators manipulate you. Let your "yes" be "yes" and your "no" be "no".

As Believers, I often wonder why we trust more in our abilities to manipulate situations and people than we believe in the capacity of God to supply all of our needs. Manipulation is rooted in deception. While explicit lies may not be told, manipulators seek to paint pictures that are designed to help them acquire what they desire. For example, some married people will withhold sex from their spouses in an attempt to overcome the will of their spouse. They will give their spouses the cold shoulder, stop speaking to their spouses, and continue to have a bad attitude with their spouses, as opposed to communicating and finding a resolution to their issues. Some Believers will use money, power, and position to override the wills of other individuals. Have you ever had someone try to make you feel guilty about a decision that you made? Someone like this may even say things like, "If you don't do it, I'll find someone who will." I've heard stories of young men suggesting to their current girlfriends the possibility of them dating other women; they did this in an attempt to get their girlfriends to compromise their purity. I've also heard stories of young women doing this to young men. In each one of these examples, the underlying theme is manipulation. Suppose a person tells us that they do not want to do something. In that case, it is our responsibility to respect that person's will and not attempt to manipulate the individual into doing what we want him or her to do.

Another example of manipulation is when people ask the same question repeatedly, even after the question has been answered. The person continues to ask the question to get us to change our answer and agree with whatever it is that they want. As Believers, we need to recognize when someone is trying to manipulate us, and we need to recognize when we are trying to manipulate others. God does not continually ask us the same question in an attempt to manipulate us. He presents options, and with our free will, we can choose what it is that we would like to do. The Word of God prompts us to choose life or death, and it also presents the option for us to choose blessings or curses (see Deuteronomy 30:19). We are not robots programmed to do what others want us to do. Even still, some people use excessive flattery and embellished compliments to manipulate us into agreeing with them.

As Believers, it is vital that we ask God for discernment and the ability to see manipulation when it appears. We also need to ask God for purity of heart, so we don't enter into manipulation and try to twist the will of others. We have to rise to the level of maturity that allows us to take the yes or no answers of other individuals and not try to further manipulate them into changing.

Day 28

Faith It Until You Make It

Hebrews 11:1 - Now faith is the substance of things hoped for, the evidence of things not seen.

Faith it into existence! Faith is the confidence that something will happen. As Believers, we walk by faith and not by sight. As Believers, we walk daily using the confidence that we have in God and that He will do what His Word says. His Word says that He will care for us, provide for us, and protect us. His Word says that healing is our portion. His Word also says that we are His beloved, and we have a special place in His heart. Throughout the Word of God, we are given specific instructions on how to walk in the blessings of God. It is made clear that without faith, it is impossible to please God.

We do ourselves a disservice when we lack confidence in the fact that God can do exceedingly and abundantly above all that we can ask or think (see Ephesians 3:20). Without faith, we cannot rise to the level of peace and abundance promised to us in the Word of God. There are thousands of promises in the Word of God that we can lay claim to by simply having faith. Let's begin by having faith that God seeks to give us the good of the land.

Having faith in the promises of God opens our lives to an immeasurable amount of goodness. As Believers, we must have faith in the fact that God is our strength. We must have faith in the fact that God will never leave us. We must have faith in the fact that God wants to prosper us. We must have faith in the fact that God hears us when we pray. We must have faith in the fact that God fights our battles and defends us when necessary. We must also have faith that God will supply us with peace, love, and a good life. We must have faith that God has adopted us as His sons and daughters. Lastly, we must certainly have faith that God loves us, even at our lowest points in life.

Faith is one of the biggest weapons we possess as Believers. Faith is confidence in

God's ability. Remember, our weapons are not carnal, but are mighty for the pulling down of strongholds. Faith can pull down the strongholds of doubt, worry, fear, and dismay. There will be many times in life where we will have to faith things into existence. We will simply have to believe God and take Him at His Word. And that's right where God wants us—in faith, not in uncertainty or disbelief. It is a choice to either walk in faith or to walk in something else - most likely fear. Some Believers go their entire lives walking in fear instead of faith. Some even die in fear and disbelief. They never received the fullness of life that God promised them. Our testimony will be different! Today, we have decided to choose faith over fear.

Day 29

Come Out Of Confusion

2 Corinthians 10:5 - Casting down imaginations, and every high thing that exalteth itself against the knowledge of God and bringing into captivity every thought to the obedience of Christ.

If God is NOT the author of confusion, could it be someone else writing the confusing chapters of our lives? Jesus is the Author and the Finisher of our faith, but why do our stories often involve confusion (see Hebrews 12:2)? God is not the author of confusion, nor is He the author of disorder (see 1 Corinthians 14:33). Nevertheless, many Believers live in a state of confusion. I have great news! We can cast down imaginations that come against our minds. We can also bring our thoughts into captivity to the obedience of Christ (see 2 Corinthians 10:5).

Our minds are one of our most valuable assets. The truth of the matter is, the enemy (Satan) knows the value of our minds. Satan is well aware that wherever the mind goes, the man or woman is sure to follow. Satan fights us so hard in our thinking. Satan knows that when we live in a state of confusion, we will make decisions that do not produce God's best results for us. Confusion causes us to make hasty decisions. It can also cause us to make decisions out of pure desperation. God wants our minds to be in sync with Him. I like to place one of my hands on my head and repeat, "Let this mind be in you (me) that was also in Christ Jesus" (Philippians 2:5).

I don't like being confused. I don't like mental chaos; it is one of the things that bothers me the most. I like order. Not in an overly rigid, legalistic way, but in a way that lays out details that make it easier to reach the intended goal. I found that when I minimize confusion, it is easier for me to obtain sweatless victories. As a business owner, I must promote and produce an environment that limits confusion; this way, I can successfully and peacefully handle matters for my clients and employees. As a ministry leader, I have to maintain an organized mind and organized methods to ensure that those who I lead consistently obtain success. As a parent, I must limit confusion because I'm leading my child toward becoming a productive member of society.

It's hard to follow a confused person. If you find yourself here, it is good to ask questions and communicate clearly about the respective goal. Law school is where I honed my ability to minimize confusion, but I believe that even before I attended law school, I was a very inquisitive person and wanted to know the next best steps. Everyone will not go to law school, but we can all practice our communication skills, including listening, critical thinking, and asking good questions.

As Believers, it's imperative that we ask questions and learn how to effectively communicate so that confusion is not invited into our lives. When forming a team or managing a project or event, we must have a clear, distinct vision and articulate that vision so that those responsible for carrying it out are aware of how to carry out the steps.

In whatever industry we work in, we do not want to get a reputation for being confused. Others may find it difficult or unbearable to work with us. In either of those instances, tasks remain undone all because of confusion. As we advance, let us make a conscious effort to reduce confusion so that we, just like Jesus, can truly be about our Father's business (see Luke 2:49).

Day 30

Final Destination

Romans 12:22 - Do not conform to the pattern of this world, but be transformed by the renewing of your mind. Then you will be able to test and approve what God's will is—his good, pleasing and perfect will.

We are transformed by the renewing of our minds. The enemy attacks the mind because the body will go wherever the mind directs it.

This world's system offers us so many things that are in direct conflict with God's will for our lives. It offers us illicit sex, illegal substances, sorcery, opportunities to walk in pride, and the list goes on and on. As Believers, it can sometimes get difficult to just live according to God's instructions and maintain some level of Christ-likeness. And we were not called to be like the world. We are a chosen generation, royal priesthood, a holy nation, a peculiar people (see 1 Peter 2:9).

It is God's will that we not be so closely identified with the ways of this world that people cannot tell us apart. Our attitudes and mindsets should be different. In this day and age, some people feel like being different is a bad thing. In actuality, when you look at most things that are considered valuable, they have a different consistency, style, or makeup. The most valuable cars are usually limited in supply. The most valuable homes usually have an eclectic, unique style.

So is the case with us as Believers. Our consistency (who we are) should be different than the status quo. Our temperaments and attitudes should reflect the peace and joy that God has gifted us. Our attitudes should be kinder and gentler than what we see most people exhibit. Our outlooks on life should be more positive as we think on those things that are lovely, pure, and of good report (see Philippians 4:8).

Jesus, our role model, was VERY different. He intended to come to this world and turn it upside down, and He was very successful at doing that. So, the question is, what are we going to do to demonstrate our uniqueness and leave a mark on this world? Will your impact be a best-selling book? Will your impact be an award-winning movie? Will your impact be a nonprofit organization or a million-dollar corporation? Will you help children in need? Will you preach to and teach those who need knowledge? Will you feed the hungry? Will you build houses for the homeless? Will you contribute to charity? Will you help your churches grow by lending them your gifts? What will your impact look like? God has called us out to be different. Will you answer the call?

Day 31

See Yourself

Matthew 7:3-5 - Why do you look at the speck of sawdust in your brother's eye and pay no attention to the plank in your own eye? How can you say to your brother, 'Let me take the speck out of your eye,' when all the time there is a plank in your own eye? You hypocrite, first take the plank out of your own eye, and then you will see clearly to remove the speck from your brother's eye.

We made it to day 31! That means that we are dedicated to changing our lives and experiencing Nothing Missing Nothing Broken.

On this last day, I want you to look back through this book and identify which days meant the most to you and which days spoke to you. Even consider reading the devotional again to soak up ALL the goodness it provides.

I also want you to consider gifting someone with their copy of this book, especially if you see them struggling with the topics we have covered.

My closing thoughts would be, always let the examination of ourselves outweigh the examination of others.

Shalom!